Reading
BOROUGH COUNCIL

Reading Borough Libraries

Email: info@readinglibraries.org.uk
Website: www.readinglibraries.org.uk

Reading 0118 9015950
Battle   0118 9015100
Caversham 0118 9015103
Palmer Park 0118 9015106
Southcote 0118 9015109
Tilehurst 0118 9015112
Whitley 0118 9015115

RoP 05/08	26. OCT 13.		
	29. APR 14.		
23. JUL 08	28. JAN 15.		
21. AUG 08	APR 15		
23. SEP 08	17. JUN 15		
02. APR 11			
26. MAR 12	13. AUG 15		
10. AUG 13	08. JUL 16		

PET

Toy Workshop
CH745.5

CHILDREN'S LIBRARY

To avoid overdue charges please return this book to a
Reading library on or before the last date stamped above.
If not required by another reader, it may be renewed by
personal visit, telephone, post, email, or via our website.

Reading Borough Council

34126002610189

D1439242

The Five Mile Press Pty Ltd
950 Stud Road, Rowville
Victoria 3178 Australia
Email: publishing@fivemile.com.au
Website: www.fivemile.com.au

Copyright © 2004 Gorg Blanc
All rights reserved

Published in 2007
Printed in China 5 4 3 2

Recycling Fun!

Toy Workshop

The Five Mile Press

Contents

1 Ladybird

Y ou are probably used to recycling paper, cardboard or plastic. But did you know that almost all materials can be recycled or reused? In this case, we will use a nutshell to make a lovely ladybird, although, with a little imagination, you can easily make other insects or animals too!

The ladybird is a beautiful insect but remember, you don't need to paint the ladybird in its original colour. You can use other colours as well to make it more eye-catching!

tools and materials

1 Glue
2 Walnut shells
3 Thin white cardboard
4 Black acrylic paint
5 Thick black permanent marker
6 Fine paintbrush
7 Scissors
8 Red acrylic paint

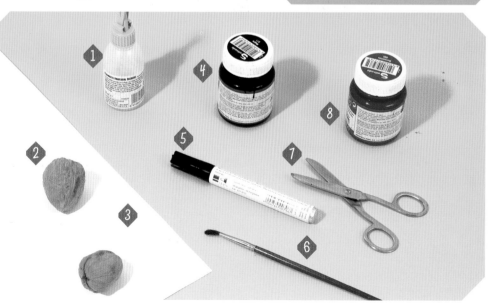

Ladybird

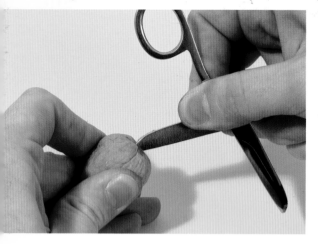

1
Open the nut without breaking the shell. Using scissors, poke them into the back part of the nut. The nut should open down the middle, and you will have two halves.

2
Once you have inserted the scissors, turn them carefully, and you will see that the nut opens up perfectly. Finish opening the nut with your own hands, making sure not to break the two halves.

3
Take one of the halves and paint it totally red. To do this, use acrylic paint diluted in a little water. If you do not dilute the paint with water, it will break once it's dry. Use a soft-bristled paintbrush, so that you can easily reach in between all of the wrinkles on the surface of the nut.

To open the nut, ask an adult for help. It is a simple operation, but if you have never done it before, it will be better if an adult helps. Once the nut shell is opened, go ahead and eat the nut!

4
Once the red acrylic paint is dry, paint a black line on the front end of the nut, as shown in the picture. The advantage of acrylic paint is that it dries quite quickly. This will allow you to paint the line an hour after you have painted the entire nut red.

5

Finish painting the entire tip of the ladybird with black acrylic paint. This will form the head of this lovely insect, where you will later stick on its eyes.

When you are working with acrylic paint, put a sheet of newspaper down to cover the work area. This will keep your work space clean.

6

Use the same black acrylic paint to paint small spots on the ladybird. Use only the tip of the paintbrush and apply very vertical brushstrokes in such a way that you leave small drops of black paint on the red shell.

While you let the paint dry ...

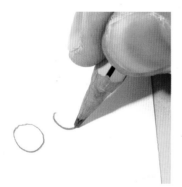

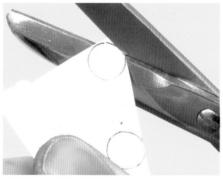

On a piece of thin white cardboard, use a pencil to draw two small circles, each measuring approximately 8 mm in diameter.

Using scissors, cut out the two circles. Because they're so small, you'll have to be careful that you cut very neatly.

Use the thick black marker to paint a dot in the middle of the two circles. Now you have made the eyes of the ladybird.

Ladybird

7

Put a drop of glue on the back of the eyes and stick them onto the top part of the area that you have painted black. Look at the picture to make sure that you have stuck the eyes on correctly.

8

Once you have stuck on the eyes and the black acrylic paint is totally dry, you will have a lovely ladybird to play with. If you want, you can put a little adhesive on the underneath of the ladybird, and stick it onto the wall or to the side of your computer screen!

2 Wooden aeroplane

The sticks that are normally used for icy poles are a great resource for making crafts, because they are wooden and very strong. If you do not eat enough icy poles to collect enough of these sticks, you can find them in craft stores.

tools and materials

1. Red paint
2. Masking tape
3. Thin black cardboard
4. Cutter
5. Scissors
6. Thumbtacks with plastic head
7. Glue
8. Black paint
9. Paintbrush
10. Bottle cork
11. Wooden matches
12. Wooden icy pole sticks
13. Pencil
14. Ruler
15. Black permanent marker

6

1 Using a cutter, slice a thin disc off one end of the cork. Ask an adult to help you do this. You must never use a cutter by yourself because it is a very sharp and dangerous tool.

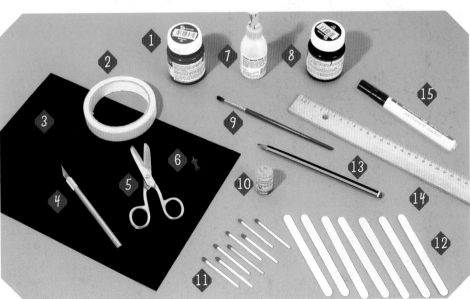

Wooden Aeroplane

2

On one of the wooden icy pole sticks, mark a line at a distance of 25 mm from each end.

3

Using scissors, cut off the two ends that you have marked on the icy pole stick. Cut right along the mark. Then paint them with red paint.

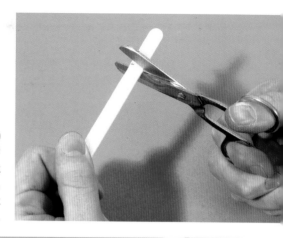

4

Now mark a 3 cm section on another icy pole stick. Make sure to include the rounded tip in your measurement.

5

Take another wooden icy pole stick and paste a drop of liquid glue on one of its ends.

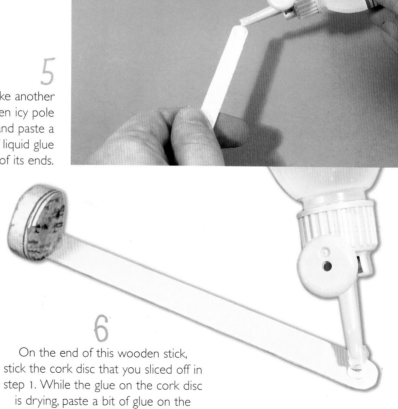

6

On the end of this wooden stick, stick the cork disc that you sliced off in step 1. While the glue on the cork disc is drying, paste a bit of glue on the other end of the wooden stick.

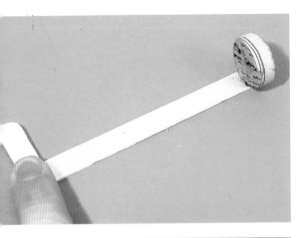

7

On the end of the stick that has the glue, stick the 3 cm piece of stick that you cut off earlier.

8

Place a drop of glue on the cork disc, as shown in this picture.

9

On the cork disc, stick another wooden icy pole stick like the one that you stuck the cork on, at the other end.

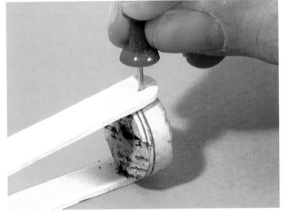

10

Use a thumbtack with a plastic head to secure the joint between the wooden stick and the cork. Poke the thumbtack into the wooden stick until it sticks into the cork disc.

11

Take two wooden icy pole sticks and paint them totally red.

Wooden Aeroplane

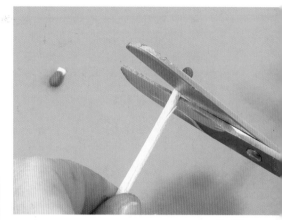

To paint the body of the aeroplane, use a fine paintbrush. Use smooth brushstrokes for an even effect.

12
While the two wooden sticks are drying, paint the body of the aeroplane that you have just made.

13
Now cut the head of a wooden match off. It is important for the match to be wooden because cardboard matches will not work for what we have to do.

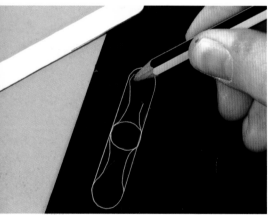

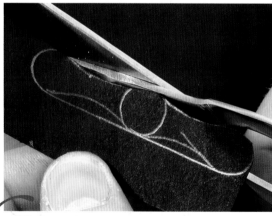

15
Carefully cut out the propeller that you have just drawn.

16
Leave a spot that is a bit wider in the middle of the propeller, so that you can later stick it to the aeroplane.

14
Trace the rounded shape of one of the wooden icy pole sticks on a piece of thin black cardboard. Inside this pattern, draw the shape of a propeller. Drawing with a normal pencil will make the lines appear bright on the black background.

17

Paste a drop of glue on each side of the body of the plane, as you can see in the picture.

When you are going to stick on the wooden sticks, which will be the wings of the plane, make sure that they are nice and centred so that the wings are an even length on both sides.

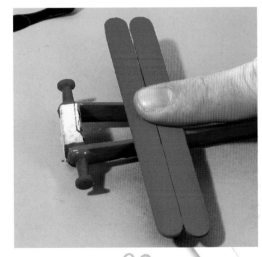

18

On the spot that you have just prepared with glue, very carefully stick one of the red painted wooden sticks.

19

Place a bit of glue next to the wooden stick that you have just stuck on the body of the plane.

20

Carefully glue the other red wooden stick next to the first stick. Using your fingertips, press down on the wooden sticks so that they stick nicely.

21

Cut a 3 cm section from the end of another wooden icy pole stick. Then, cut another 3 cm section from the other end.

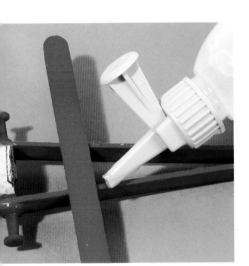

Wooden Aeroplane

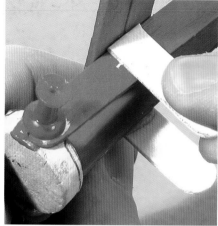

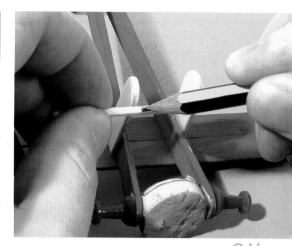

22

Using some liquid glue, stick each piece you have just cut onto the body of the plane – right below the wings, as shown.

23

Using your fingertips, press down on the wooden pieces so that they stick well to the body of the plane.

24

Once you have stuck on the wooden pieces, take the match that you prepared earlier, and mark on it the distance between the two wooden sticks that you have just stuck on.

Ask an adult to help you whenever you use the cutter.

Paint every side of the cork.

26

Cut off two thin discs from a bottle cork. Then, use a black permanent marker to paint them.

25

Using scissors, cut the match the same size as the distance that separates the two wooden pieces.

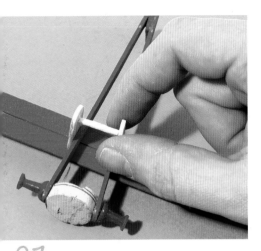

27

Stick the piece of match between the two wooden pieces that you have stuck onto the body of the plane.

28

Poke a thumbtack through the middle of the cork discs that you have just painted with the marker.

29

Now, poke the thumbtack through the wooden stick and the match, as shown in the picture. Make sure when you do this that none of the pieces become unglued.

30

Once you have attached the two wheels to the bottom of the plane, paint black the two wooden pieces that you have joined together with the match.

31

Use the same black paint to add a few details onto the cork disc at the front of the plane.

Wooden Aeroplane

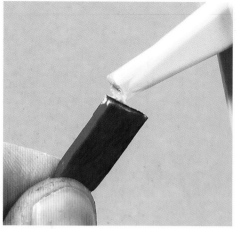

32

Take the two 2.5 cm wooden pieces of stick that you painted red at the beginning of this exercise and paste a little glue on the flat tip of each of them.

33

Very carefully stick one of these wooden pieces onto the tail of the plane. This will be the aileron of the aeroplane.

34

Stick the other piece on the other side of the tail of the plane. Hold it in place until the glue has dried.

35

Use a thumbtack to attach the propeller to the centre of the cork at the front of the plane.

If you want to make sure that the thumbtacks stick firmly, paste a drop of glue on their tips before you poke them into the plane.

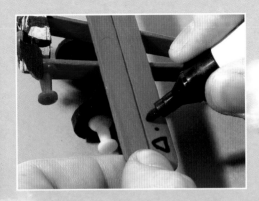

36

With a permanent marker, draw some numbers or an insignia on the wings. Use your imagination!

37

Let the plane dry properly before you fly it all around the air space of your room. Now you have your own classic wooden plane! If you want, you can build a biplane by simply adding wings onto the bottom of the plane.

3 Picture of a Ski Lift

Cardboard is very easy to recycle and plays a central role in toymaking because it allows us to do so many things. Here you will learn how to make a three-dimensional picture of a gondola ski lift that you can run. See the effect that is created by having the picture in relief – it will look like you have a window open overlooking a ski resort!

1

Trace the shape of a sheet of a paper on a piece of thick cardboard. If you use a piece of brown cardboard, you can save yourself from having to paint the mountains in the picture.

Tools and materials

1. Liquid glue
2. Several colours of paint
3. Thin white, blue and black cardboard
4. Paintbrush
5. Pencil
6. Thick black marker
7. Ruler
8. Scissors
9. Adhesive tape
10. Nails
11. Hammer
12. Wooden board
13. String
14. Thick cardboard

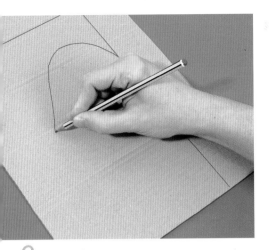

2

On the cardboard rectangle that you have just outlined, draw a mountain about the same height as the sheet of paper, but make sure not to go above this height. To give the picture more relief, this mountain must be placed to one side of the sheet, and its width must be the same as the width of the sheet.

3

Using scissors, cut this mountain out of the cardboard. Now, draw two more mountains: a medium-sized one and another shorter one. Each mountain will be placed in a different spot on the picture.

4

On a thin piece of cardboard, trace the silhouette of the tallest mountain so that you can cut out a shape that looks like a white, snow-capped peak.

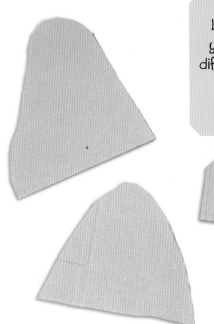

Look at the three shapes that you have cut out. They will have different heights, but the bases of all three should have the same width as the sheet of paper.

Picture of a Ski Lift

5

On another piece of thin cardboard, trace the top section of the silhouette of the medium-sized mountain. You will need to trace about 5 or 6 cm for the silhouette of the mountain.

Once you have finished cutting, you will have the three sections of mountain silhouettes. Make sure that each one is a different height.

6

Finally, on another piece of thin cardboard, trace the silhouette of the shortest mountain. Make this one shorter than the others, but make it wider horizontally, as shown in the picture.

7

Use scissors to cut out the silhouettes of the mountains that you have just drawn onto the thin white cardboard.

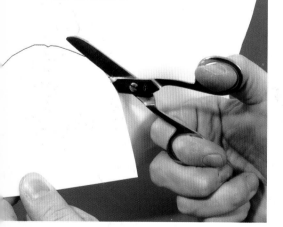

8

Take the wood that you will use as the base of the picture and trace its shape on a thin sky-blue piece of cardboard.

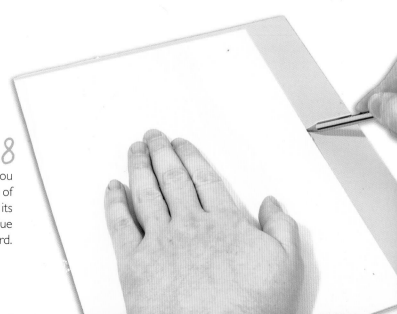

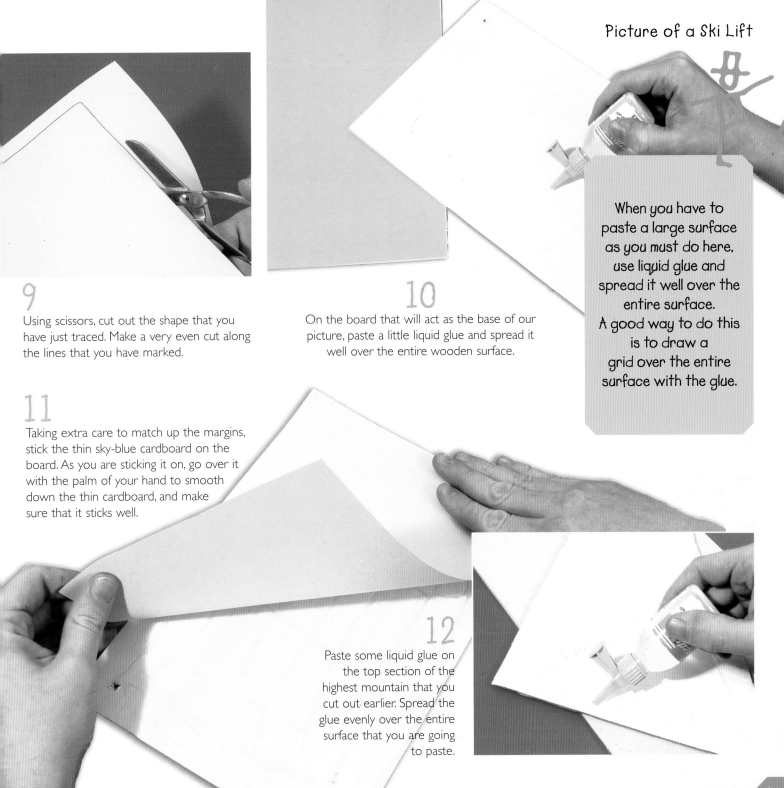

When you have to paste a large surface as you must do here, use liquid glue and spread it well over the entire surface. A good way to do this is to draw a grid over the entire surface with the glue.

9

Using scissors, cut out the shape that you have just traced. Make a very even cut along the lines that you have marked.

10

On the board that will act as the base of our picture, paste a little liquid glue and spread it well over the entire wooden surface.

11

Taking extra care to match up the margins, stick the thin sky-blue cardboard on the board. As you are sticking it on, go over it with the palm of your hand to smooth down the thin cardboard, and make sure that it sticks well.

12

Paste some liquid glue on the top section of the highest mountain that you cut out earlier. Spread the glue evenly over the entire surface that you are going to paste.

Picture of a Ski Lift

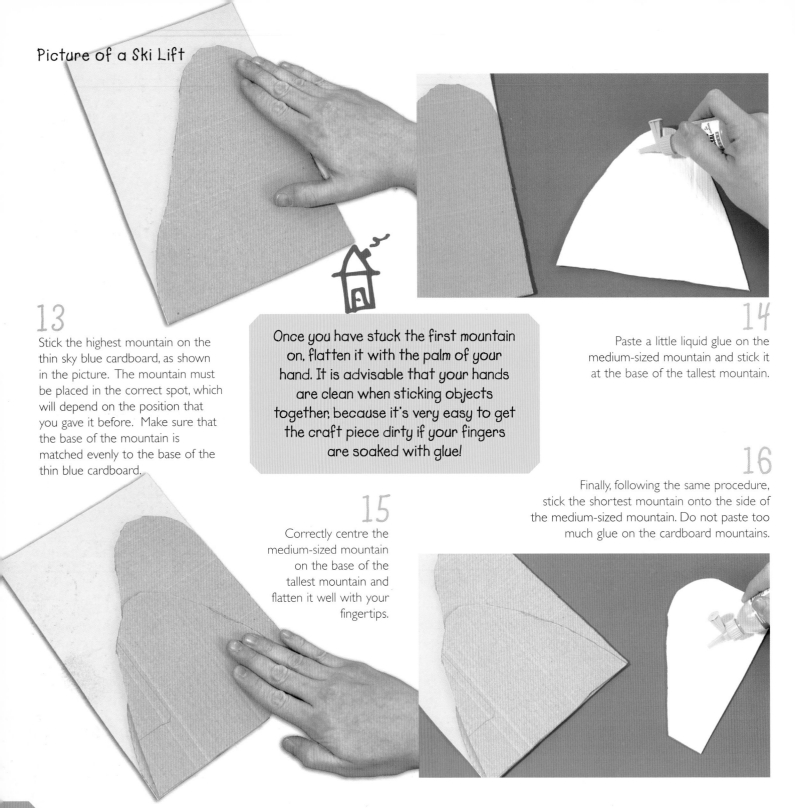

13

Stick the highest mountain on the thin sky blue cardboard, as shown in the picture. The mountain must be placed in the correct spot, which will depend on the position that you gave it before. Make sure that the base of the mountain is matched evenly to the base of the thin blue cardboard.

Once you have stuck the first mountain on, flatten it with the palm of your hand. It is advisable that your hands are clean when sticking objects together, because it's very easy to get the craft piece dirty if your fingers are soaked with glue!

14

Paste a little liquid glue on the medium-sized mountain and stick it at the base of the tallest mountain.

15

Correctly centre the medium-sized mountain on the base of the tallest mountain and flatten it well with your fingertips.

16

Finally, following the same procedure, stick the shortest mountain onto the side of the medium-sized mountain. Do not paste too much glue on the cardboard mountains.

17

Centre and flatten all of the three mountains. Now you can see that the three pieces are superimposed in such a way that they look like they are in relief.

18

Take the thin white cardboard silhouettes, and cut their bottom parts, to give them a wavy shape so that it will look like the mountains are snow-capped.

19

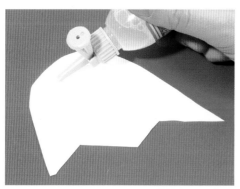

Paste some liquid glue on the top part of the snow-capped silhouettes. Paste only a tiny bit of glue, so that the thin cardboard does not wrinkle from the moisture.

The snow-capped silhouette of the smallest mountain must not be very wavy, because it snows less on the shorter mountains and so there is less snow.

20

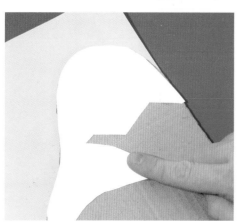

Stick the silhouettes on in the same order as you have stuck on the mountains. As you are pasting them down, make sure that they match up nicely with the shape of the mountain tops.

The landscape should look like this.

Picture of a Ski Lift

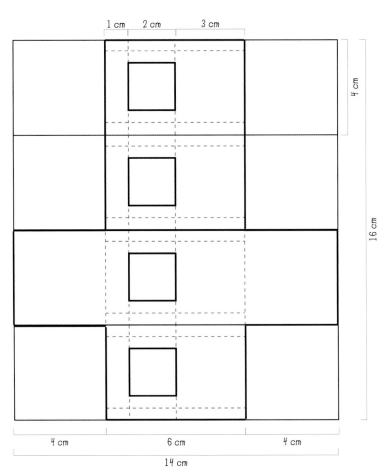

Layout of the cabin

1 cm   2 cm   3 cm

4 cm

16 cm

4 cm   6 cm   4 cm

14 cm

21

Now, take a piece of thin cardboard and mark a 16 cm line on it using a pencil and a ruler.

To draw the gondola cabin, you must draw and mark a design on the cardboard like the one that you see in the pictures. You can use the attached pattern, so that you can better see how to draw this piece.

22

Using the first line that you have drawn, trace a 16 by 14 cm rectangle. Use the side of the cardboard, so that you do not have to cut out all of the sides of the rectangle.

23

On the 16 cm sides mark four dots that are 4 cm apart from each other. On the 14 cm side, mark one dot 4 cm from one corner, another dot 6 cm from the last dot, and another dot 4 cm from the corner opposite to the one you have first marked.

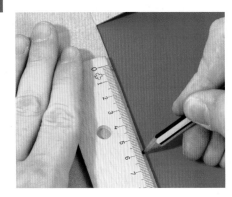

24

Using scissors, cut out the shape on the cardboard that you have just drawn. Make sure that you do not confuse the cutting lines with the reference lines.

25

Your cardboard shape should look like this.

26

On each side of the shape, mark lines that are at a distance of 1 cm from each side. On these lines, make a mark at a distance of 1 cm from the top and another mark at a distance of 3 cm from the bottom. Now, make a mark at a distance of 1 cm from the edge and another one at a distance of 2 cm from the last mark.

27

Make these marks at both ends of the cross shape and connect them by drawing a straight line that goes across the cardboard cross. Draw the lines that connect the spots marked every 4 cm on the cross and draw another line 1 cm from the edge of each side of the cross.

28

Cut out the windows of the ski lift and fold all of the sides, so that they take on the shape of the cabin.

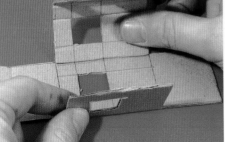

29

Stick a piece of adhesive tape onto one side flap of the ski lift, so that you can stick it to the opposite side.

Picture of a Ski Lift

30
Fold the sides of the ski lift so that the adhesive tape stays hidden inside the piece of cardboard. When you are sticking the sides of the gondola cabin together, make sure that the cabin looks aligned and square.

31
Now fold the bottom of the ski lift and stick a little adhesive tape on it. Once you have perfectly closed up the ski lift, except for the top part, you can begin to paint it.

32
Use a medium paintbrush and yellow or red paint, depending on what you prefer. Completely paint the ski lift. Use long brushstrokes and always apply the paint in the same direction, so that there is no trace of the brushstrokes.

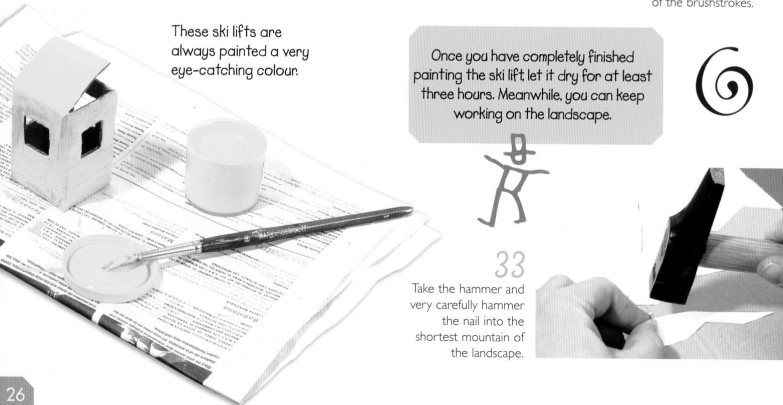

These ski lifts are always painted a very eye-catching colour.

Once you have completely finished painting the ski lift, let it dry for at least three hours. Meanwhile, you can keep working on the landscape.

33
Take the hammer and very carefully hammer the nail into the shortest mountain of the landscape.

34

Hammer another nail into the top of the highest mountain of the landscape, so that between the two tails you could draw a slanted imaginary line.

35

Use the side and front of the ski lift as a reference to cut four pieces of thin blue cardboard. Make these pieces a little narrower than each side of the ski lift.

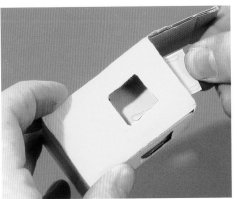

36

Paste some liquid glue on the ends of each piece of thin cardboard that you have cut out. Very carefully insert each piece of thin cardboard and stick them onto the windows of the ski lift. The glue must not show on the window openings.

38

Using a black permanent marker, draw a frame around each window, the door, and any other detail that improves the appearance of the ski lift.

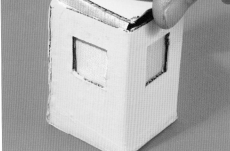

37

Once you have stuck the four windows on, place a little adhesive tape on the top part of the gondola cabin and close it, as shown in the picture.

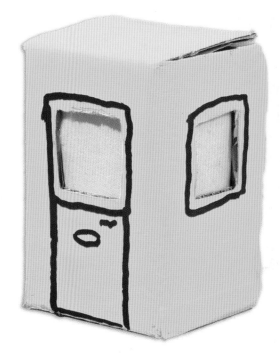

Picture of a Ski Lift

39

Cut a 10 by 3 cm rectangle out of thin black cardboard and fold it in half. Once you have folded it, cut out the shape, making the base wider – that is to say, the end where the two sides are not connected, so that the end where the two sides are still connected is narrower.

Once you have finished cutting, fold out the last 1 cm of each one of the ends where the sides are not connected as shown.

40

Paste some liquid glue in the middle of this piece of thin black cardboard, so that both sides stick together perfectly. Also, paste some glue on the bottom ends that you have folded out, so that you can stick the piece on top of the ski lift.

41

Stick the piece of thin black cardboard on the middle of the ski lift roof. Make a hole at the top of the cardboard and tie a piece of string in a knot around this hole.

42

Without cutting the string, place the ski lift between the two nails and use the string to measure twice the distance between both nails. Feed the string around the two nails and tie the ends of the string together.

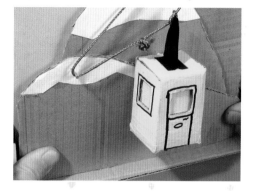

Picture of a Ski Lift

44

Cut a piece of thick cardboard that is as long as the base of our alpine landscape. Paste a little glue on the end of this piece, which must be at least 10 cm wide, and on top of the line of glue, stick the snow-capped landscape that you have just created. This way you will have a stand to hold up your landscape.

43

Paste some liquid glue onto the top part of the thin blue cardboard, so that you can stick a cotton cloud on it.

45

Let the glue dry and you will have a postcard of a high mountain landscape in relief. If you use the string carefully, you will see how the ski lift moves up and down the mountains.

Submarine Periscope

A periscope is one of the most fun objects that we can build at home. It is a type of cardboard tube that we can use to see things from a different height than the one we are at. So, if we hide behind a couch and we want to look over the top of it without being seen, the two mirrors that make up the periscope will allow us to see what is going on on the other side of the couch.

1

Take the rectangular box and draw a line down the centre of it. To do this, mark all four sides in the centre, and join them together. Now, take the box apart, because you are going to cut it down this centre line.

Tools and materials

1 Rectangular cardboard box
2 Two small mirrors
3 Thin black cardboard
4 Ruler
5 Paintbrushes
6 Pencil
7 Black permanent marker
8 Liquid glue
9 Adhesive tape
10 White and blue paint
11 Cutter
12 Scissors

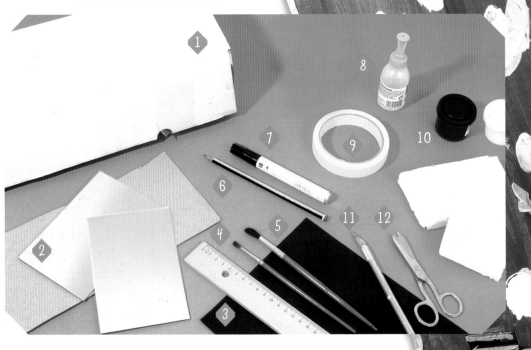

3

Take one of the box halves and, starting at one end of the box, measure off a distance of 30 cm and make a mark.

2

Using scissors, cut the box into two identical halves. To cut the box, ask an adult for help because, apart from helping you to avoid any danger, he or she will be able to cut with stronger scissors than ours.

4

Paint the cardboard box with blue paint. To do this, you must use a medium paintbrush and have the cardboard completely unfolded, so that you do not leave any parts unpainted.

Once you have painted the two parts of the cardboard box the same colour blue, let them dry before you continue working.

5

Mark a slanted line on the inner flaps of the cardboard as shown, so that it does not interfere with the space intended for the mirror that you are going to mount in the box.

Submarine Periscope

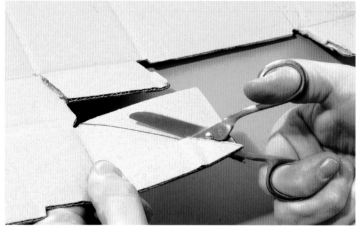

Reassemble the cardboard box and, on the inside, mark the position of the slanted flaps that you have just cut.

6

Using scissors, cut the cardboard along the line that you have just marked, as shown in the picture.

9

Put the box together again and secure the flaps with a piece of adhesive tape.

With adhesive tape, the flaps will not move when you insert the mirror through the opening that you have made with the cutter.

8

Take the box apart and use the shortest edge of the mirror to finish marking the spot on the inside of the box, where you are going to mount the mirror.

Ask an adult for help using a cutter to cut along the line you have just marked.

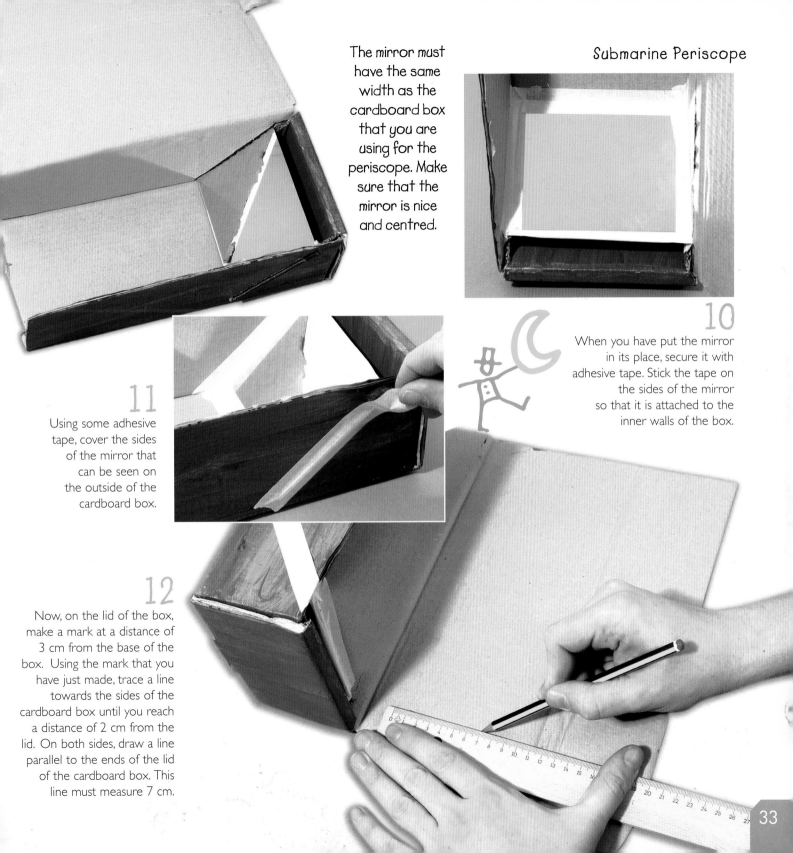

The mirror must have the same width as the cardboard box that you are using for the periscope. Make sure that the mirror is nice and centred.

10

When you have put the mirror in its place, secure it with adhesive tape. Stick the tape on the sides of the mirror so that it is attached to the inner walls of the box.

11

Using some adhesive tape, cover the sides of the mirror that can be seen on the outside of the cardboard box.

12

Now, on the lid of the box, make a mark at a distance of 3 cm from the base of the box. Using the mark that you have just made, trace a line towards the sides of the cardboard box until you reach a distance of 2 cm from the lid. On both sides, draw a line parallel to the ends of the lid of the cardboard box. This line must measure 7 cm.

Submarine Periscope

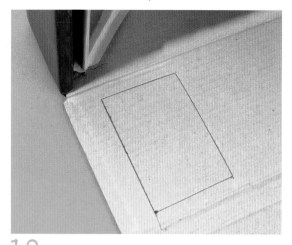

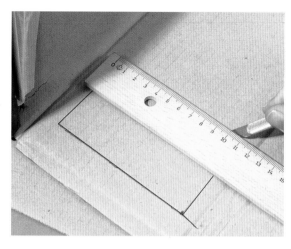

14

Ask an adult for help using the cutter, and cut out the cardboard rectangle that you have just drawn.

13

Once you have drawn all of the lines, you should have an 11 cm by 17 cm rectangle drawn on the lids of the cardboard box.

16

Cut the parts of the cardboard that are double layered. Only cut one of the two parts, so that this cut part of the periscope will be able to enter into the other part.

15

Take one of the two parts of the periscope and, once you have closed it, make a 10 cm cut into its corners.

17

Cut the corners of the cardboard on the opposite end to where you have mounted the mirror. This cut must be made at an angle, which will allow you to fold the cardboard a little.

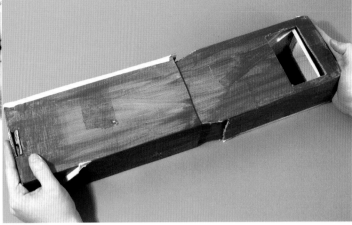

18

Using a little adhesive tape, seal the cardboard box closed before you put one piece inside the other.

19

Very carefully insert the piece that you have cut inside the other part of the periscope. Slide the one part of the periscope into the other until it is nice and secure inside the other. Do not force the cardboard boxes too much, or you might break them.

When you connect the two parts of the box together, each mirror must be facing a different way – one forwards and the other one backwards.

Insert the two pieces until you feel them reach their limit. This limit will most likely be the spot where you have stopped cutting the double layers of the cardboard box.

20

Secure the spot where both pieces of the periscope meet, by wrapping it with a little adhesive tape.

21

Stick adhesive tape around the periscope as straight as possible.

Submarine Periscope

22

Take a piece of thin black cardboard and cut a rectangular piece, the sides of which are 1 cm wider than the opening you have made earlier. The thin black cardboard rectangle must measure 13 cm by 9 cm.

To stick the tape on well, you must have a piece that measures the same as each side of the rectangle. Stick half of the piece of tape on the outside, and the other half inside the hole. Also, cover the sides of the openings for the mirrors.

23

Stick a little adhesive tape on each side of the rectangular hole through which you can see the periscope mirror. By doing this, you will make sure that the mirror does not move and that the ribbed cardboard does not show.

24

Once you have covered the holes with adhesive tape, paste a little glue on the frame of the rectangle that you have just covered.

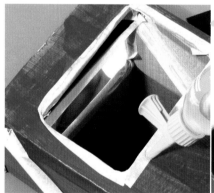

25

Out of the thin black cardboard rectangle, cut an 11 cm by 7 cm interior rectangle to create a frame like the one that appears in the picture. If you want, you can leave an extra 1 or 2 cm on one of the longer sides – that is to say, the 11 cm sides – to act as a sunshade.

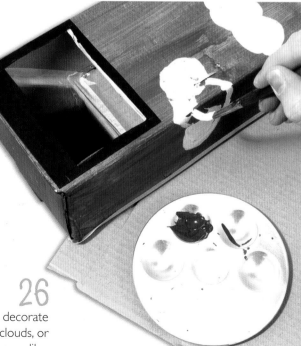

26

Using a little white paint, decorate the periscope with clouds, or whatever you like.

Let the paint on the periscope dry for at least 2 hours before you begin looking through it.

27

You can now use your periscope to observe things at a different height without being seen yourself. If you use it with imagination, you can have a lot of fun playing submarines or spy games. Have fun!

5 Nice Grasshopper

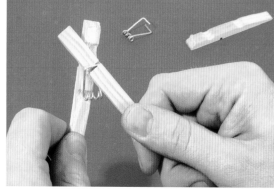

In this exercise we will show you how to build a grasshopper out of pegs. The grasshopper is quite a complicated insect because its back legs must be very long and strong, and you will have to stick them very carefully on a regular peg. We have painted the grasshopper green, but you can paint it any colour you like.

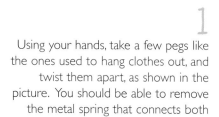

1

Using your hands, take a few pegs like the ones used to hang clothes out, and twist them apart, as shown in the picture. You should be able to remove the metal spring that connects both pieces together.

Tools and materials

1 Liquid glue
2 Wooden pegs
3 Scissors
4 Light green acrylic paint
5 Thumbtacks with plastic head
6 Small wooden sticks
7 Paintbrush
8 Pencil
9 Thin green cardboard
10 Permanent marker

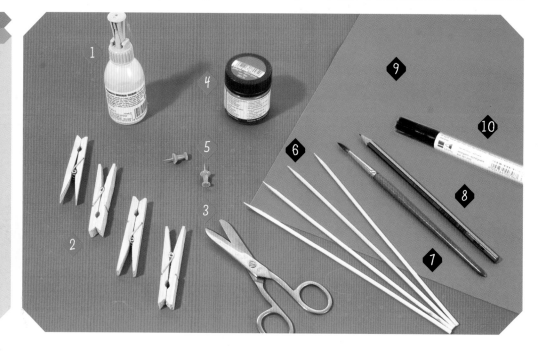

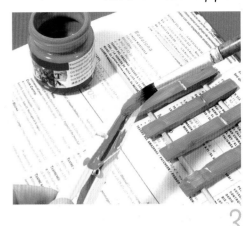

When you have finished painting the pieces, clean the paintbrush immediately and dry it with some toilet paper or an old rag. This will prevent the paint from drying on the paintbrush which will make it last longer.

2

Using a medium paintbrush paint each half of the pegs green. To do this, use paint diluted in a tiny bit of water.

3

Once you have painted the peg halves, take another whole peg and paint it with green paint as well.

4

Once you have painted all the pieces, place them over two small wooden sticks to dry, as shown in the picture. Let them dry for at least three hours.

5

Using a little liquid glue, stick one of the peg halves on the whole peg, in such a way that the peg half is tilted upward and outward. Paste a little glue on the back part of the peg half and stick it on in such a way that the sharper end is tilted upward.

When you are working with glue and you get your fingers dirty, clean them immediately. A lot of dirt can get stuck to the glue on your fingers, and this dirt can get our grasshopper dirty!

6

Paste a little glue on the intact peg right next to where you have stuck on the last peg half. On this spot stick the other green peg half. Very carefully press down on it until the pieces stick together nicely.

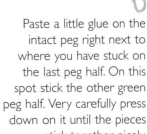

Nice Grasshopper

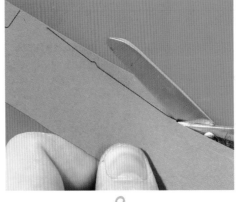

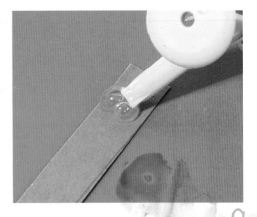

7
Trace the shape of a wooden peg on the thin green cardboard, and then fold it lengthwise to make a long strip.

8
Use scissors to cut out the strip and make one of its ends pointed.

9
Paste some liquid glue on the flat end of the thin green cardboard strip and spread it a little.

10
Cut out another thin cardboard strip exactly like the last one, and stick both of them at the end of the green peg halves that jut out of the grasshopper's body.

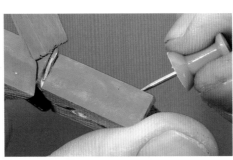

11
In the front of the intact peg, poke two thumbtacks with a green plastic head, one in each side of the wooden piece.

To poke the thumbtacks into the peg, ask an adult for help. He or she will be able do this with just his or her hands. Now you have two beady eyes!

12
Fold down the thin cardboard strips that you have stuck on before. The exact spot where you will fold the strips is at a distance of 1 cm from the tip of each peg half.

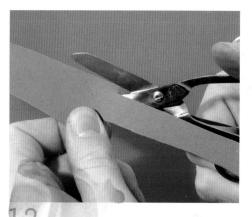

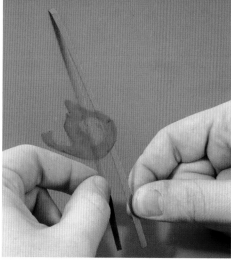

15

Fold the pieces of thin cardboard in half again, so that you get four identical strips.

13

Using scissors, cut a long and very thin strip from the thin green cardboard. This strip must measure between 20 cm and 25 cm.

14

Fold the strip exactly in half to obtain two identical pieces.

16

Using scissors, cut the four identical pieces apart. On one end of each of the strips, cut a pointed tip to better resemble the back legs of the grasshopper.

17

Paste a little glue under the intact piece, which is supporting the grasshopper structure, right below the spot where you have stuck on the two green peg halves.

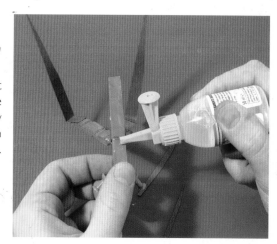

Very carefully stick the four legs on the spot that you have prepared with liquid glue. Put two legs on each side of the grasshopper.

Nice Grasshopper

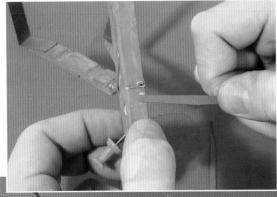

18
Now that the four legs are stuck onto the body, bend the front legs forward and the back legs backward.

19
Now you have an original wooden grasshopper to place among the flowers in your house or surprise visitors – or play a joke on your friends!

6 Toy House

When making crafts, you can quite easily create scale models, like this toy house. It will be much more gratifying if we use the building where we live or the holiday house where we have spent the summer for our model. In this case, we will make a scale copy – that is to say, a smaller copy – of a house on the canals of Amsterdam, a city in the Netherlands.

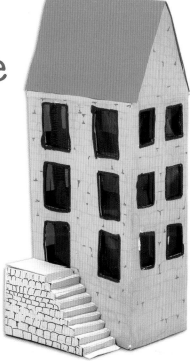

Tools and materials

1   Liquid glue
2   Thin corrugated cardboard
3   White glue
4   Several colours of thin cardboard
5   Several colours of paint
6   Paintbrush
7   Scissors
8   Cutter
9   Pencil
10 Fine tip marker
11 Thick marker
12 Adhesive tape
13 Tetra Brick carton
14 Blue cellophane paper
15 Ruler
16 Markers

1

Take the Tetra Brick and clean it well, so that you can work with it. Ask an adult to help you cut off the top of the container with a cutter.

Toy House

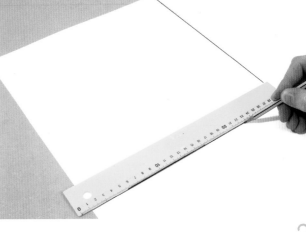

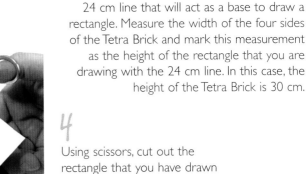

2

Cut the Tetra Brick 4 cm from the top, as shown in the picture.

When you are measuring, move the pencil with precision along each side so that you are not off by so much as a millimetre.

3

On a piece of thin white cardboard, draw a 24 cm line that will act as a base to draw a rectangle. Measure the width of the four sides of the Tetra Brick and mark this measurement as the height of the rectangle that you are drawing with the 24 cm line. In this case, the height of the Tetra Brick is 30 cm.

4

Using scissors, cut out the rectangle that you have drawn on the thin white cardboard.

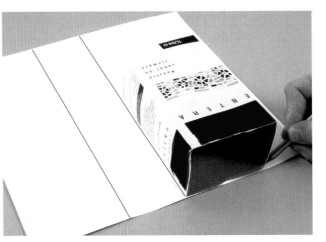

5

On the thin cardboard, mark the dimensions of the four sides of the container. This is where the cardboard will be folded.

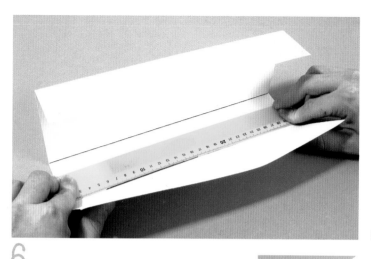

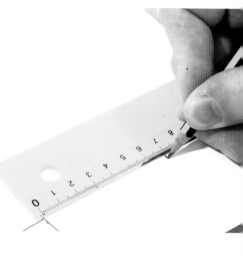

7

Make a mark on each of the folding lines at a distance of 7 cm away from the mark you made to indicate the height of the Tetra Brick.

6

With the help of a ruler, fold the thin cardboard, as if it were the sides of the Tetra Brick.

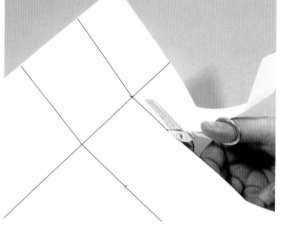

8

Cut off the part of the thin cardboard that lies above the marks that you have just made.

10

With the help of a ruler, find the centre of the short side, which will be at a distance of 3 cm, and make a mark.

9

Using scissors, cut the thin cardboard along the folding lines that you have marked. Start cutting from the top of the thin cardboard and stop at the mark indicating the height of the Tetra Brick. Once you have made the cut, you will have four pieces of thin cardboard, two short pieces and two long pieces, which are for each side of the Tetra Brick.

45

Toy House

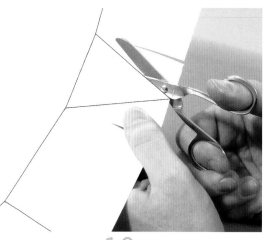

Make sure that the two triangles have the right position and size before you continue working. To check this, use a ruler and a pencil.

11

Trace a diagonal line that connects the centre of the short flaps to the point that marks the height of the Tetra Brick on the folding lines. Doing this, you will draw the triangle for the front and back part of the roof.

12

Cut off the thin cardboard that lies outside the triangle but only up to the end of the short sides – that is to say, do not cut the pieces of thin cardboard that are for the longer sides of the Tetra Brick.

13

On the thin cardboard, cut out both sides of the triangles for the short sides.

14

With the help of a ruler, fold the parts for the long sides of the Tetra Brick at the top of the thin white cardboard.

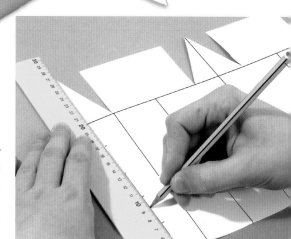

15

With a ruler, find the exact centre of each side, and divide them vertically in four sections.

16
Once you have vertically divided each side into four identical sections, divide them horizontally into 4 cm sections.

17
Take a piece of thin red cardboard and draw a 4 cm by 2 cm rectangle. Use scissors to cut it out.

18
Using the lines that you have marked on the thin white cardboard for the long, lateral sides of the Tetra Brick, mark six windows on each side. Make these marks in the centre of the top three quarters indicated earlier.

You can cut one side of the thin red cardboard rectangle to make it smaller. This way, the windows on the side of the house will be a different size than those on the front.

Once you have finished marking, the thin white cardboard should look similar to the one in the picture.

19
Paste a little liquid glue on one side of the Tetra Brick and stick the side of the thin white cardboard on the side that it matches up to on the Tetra Brick.

Toy House

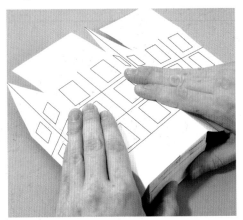

20
Using your hands, lightly press down on the Tetra Brick before you begin sticking down the rest of the thin cardboard.

21
Very carefully fold and stick all of the sides of the thin cardboard on the matching sides of the Tetra Brick carton.

Check the state of the thin cardboard once you have finished sticking it on. Let the glue dry for a while before you continue working.

Prepare a white and brown mixture to obtain a light-brown colour that looks like the colour of bricks!

23
With a fine medium paintbrush, very carefully paint the spaces between the windows of the building.

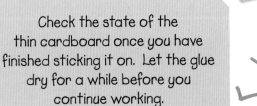

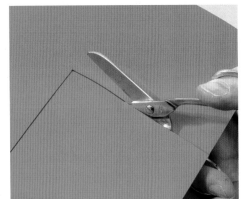

22
On a piece of thin red cardboard, draw a 9 cm by 16 cm rectangle and cut it out with scissors. This will be the roof.

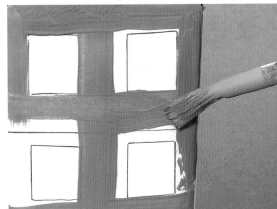

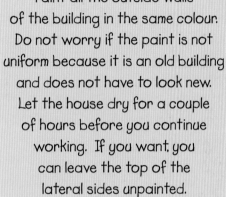

Paint all the outside walls of the building in the same colour. Do not worry if the paint is not uniform because it is an old building and does not have to look new. Let the house dry for a couple of hours before you continue working. If you want, you can leave the top of the lateral sides unpainted.

If the cellophane hangs a little over at the top of building, it is not a problem. Once you have put the roof on, it will not show.

24

Once it is dry, ask an adult for help using the cutter to cut out the spaces for the windows.

25

Take a sheet of blue cellophane paper and cut four pieces which are about the same size as each side of the building.

26

On the inside of the Tetra Brick, stick the pieces of cellophane paper using liquid glue. Do not paste glue on the spots where the cellophane must cover the windows.

27

Paste a little adhesive tape on one of the long halves at the top of the building. Stick on the tape as shown in the picture, that is to say, from the inside out.

Toy House

28

Slightly fold the adhesive tape that you have just put on and use it to stick together the two halves of the building's roof.

29

Once you have stuck the two sides of the top of the building together, stick a little more adhesive tape on to secure the two parts in place.

30

Using your fingertips, fold the adhesive tape that you have just stuck at the top of the building.

31

Take the red rectangle, which you made out of thin cardboard earlier, and fold it in half. Cover the entire surface with glue, so that the roof stays glued to the house.

Use your hands to press down a little on the roof, so that it sticks nicely.

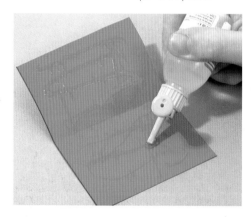

32

Using a permanent black marker, draw the window frames on the thin painted cardboard.

33

Using a light-brown marker draw the shapes of the bricks on the entire building. You must draw the bricks with a brown colour very similar to the one that you have used to paint the house because the bricks must not stand out too much.

34

Using a dark-brown marker, add details to some of the bricks that you have just drawn.

As you are making your building, check the pictures here to make sure that your model building is taking on the right appearance.

Normally, some dirt accumulates between the bricks of a building, which makes them more visible.

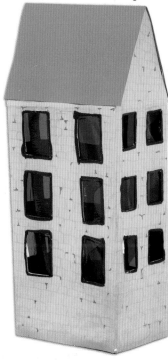

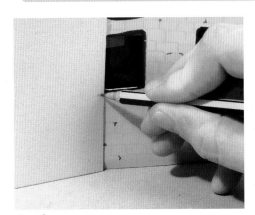

35

Now, take a piece of thin corrugated cardboard and mark on it the height of the first window.

36

Out of the cardboard cut a strip with the same width as the height of the first window.

38

Starting from the narrow side of the strip, make a mark every 5 mm.

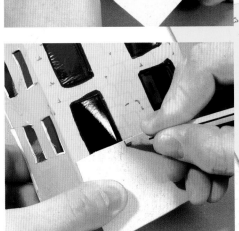

37

Put the strip on the building at the height of the first window, matching the end of the cardboard with the end of one of the sides of the building.

Toy House

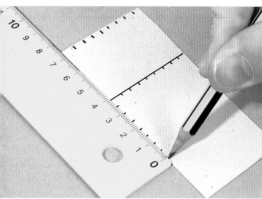

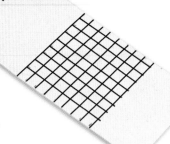

39
Repeat this process with the middle and side part of the piece of cardboard.

40
Once you have made all of the marks, connect them with straight lines, forming a grid like the one shown in the picture.

41
Using scissors, very carefully cut this grid in half at a diagonal – that is to say, you must start at the first square on one end of the grid and terrace or 'step up' as you are cutting.

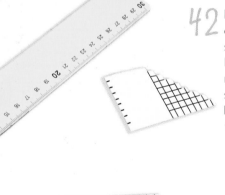

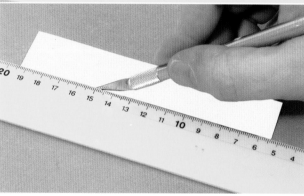

42
Prepare another strip of thin corrugated cardboard the same width as the last one but longer. On this strip, mark the same distance that separates the end of the building from the end of the window, and, starting from this mark, draw vertical lines every 5 mm on the strip of cardboard.

43
With the help of an adult, scratch the cardboard strip with a cutter. You can make this scratch down the long side of the strip, 4 cm in from the edge.

44
Using scissors cut along the same spot where you have made the scratch with the cutter, but only along the scratched part. Remove the scratched piece from the strip of cardboard.

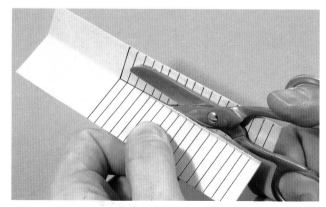

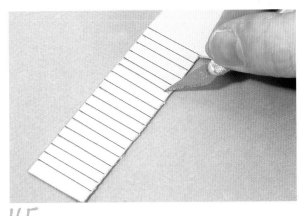

Scratching with a cutter means that you do not make a full cut. Rather, what it does is make it easier for you to fold a material like cardboard in this case.

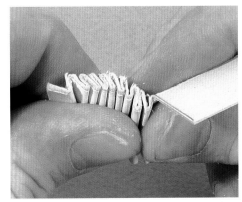

45

Using the cutter scratch the cardboard strip again along the parallel lines that you have drawn every 5 mm.

46

Fold the scratched part as if it were an accordion, that is to say, at each fold, reverse the direction in which you folded last.

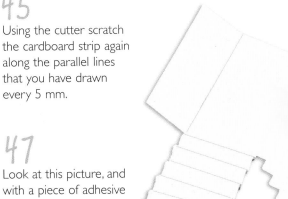

47

Look at this picture, and with a piece of adhesive tape connect the two pieces of cardboard that you have just folded and cut. Stick them together as shown in the picture.

48

Once you have mounted the piece for the staircase, connect its sides from the inside with adhesive paper tape until the structure is closed.

49

With a black marker, draw on one side of the staircase brick shapes like the ones that you made before for the building.

Stick the structure of the staircase to the building, matching the top of the piece up with the window on the side of the house.

50
Once the glue is dry, you will have a fantastic model house to make your car games more interesting!

1

Indian Teepee

Indian teepees are triangular tents. You can build a very realistic Indian teepee out of pointed wooden sticks such as kebab skewers, plus a little cardboard.

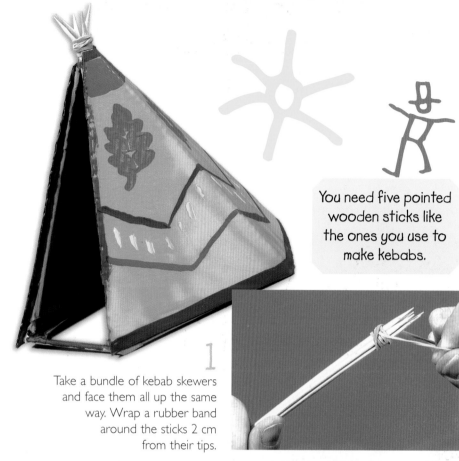

You need five pointed wooden sticks like the ones you use to make kebabs.

1

Take a bundle of kebab skewers and face them all up the same way. Wrap a rubber band around the sticks 2 cm from their tips.

Tools and materials

1. Several colours of paint
2. Cardboard
3. Compass
4. Cutter
5. Scissors
6. Ruler
7. Kebab skewers
8. Paintbrush
9. Adhesive tape
10. Liquid glue
11. Several different coloured permanent markers
12. Thin white cardboard
13. Pencil
14. Decorated rubber stamp
15. Rubber band

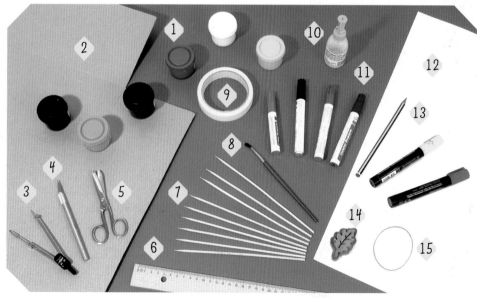

Indian Teepee

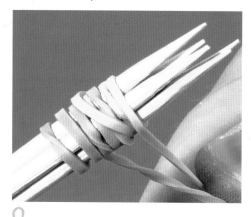

2

Tie the rubber band around the sticks by wrapping and tightening it as shown in the picture.

3

Take some more wooden sticks and measure off a 10 cm segment, which does not include the tips of the sticks.

4

Cut five 10 cm segments from the wooden sticks and stick four of them on a piece of adhesive tape each. You must stick these sticks near the edge of the tape, leaving a wide section of the tape free, as shown in the picture.

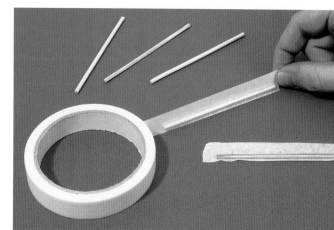

5

Take the bundle of five wooden sticks, which you have tied together with a rubber band, and separate two of them. You will have to stick the ends of these two sticks to one of the segments that you have prepared with adhesive tape. Observe the picture to do this task.

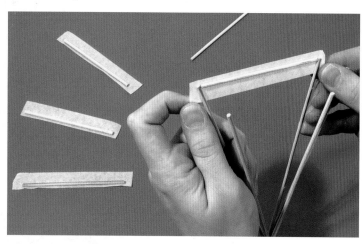

Stick on the four stick segments prepared with tape in such a way that you get four sections in the shape of a triangle.

6

Make sure that the segments that you have just added are firmly secured to the wooden sticks that you have wrapped together with a rubber band. Do not stick the tape over the middle open space, but do make sure that all of the pieces are nice and secure.

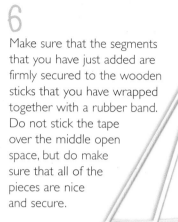

Finally, stick the 10 cm stick in the last free space. To secure it in place, stick a little adhesive tape on the edges of this last wooden stick.

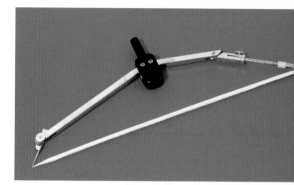

7

Take the compass and open it up to the same length as the kebab skewers that you have used to create the teepee structure.

8

Trace a circle with the same radius as the length of the wooden sticks, as shown in the picture.

9

In the centre of the circle, trace another circle with a 2 cm radius.

10

Without lifting the compass from the centre of the circle, draw a straight line that passes through the exact centre of the two circles.

Indian Teepee

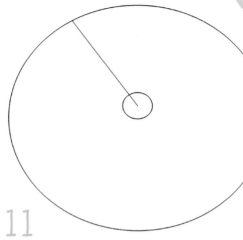

11
Once you have drawn these circumferences and lines, you should have a disc like the one that appears in the picture.

12
Using scissors, cut out the exterior circumference. Although you should cut along the line you have traced, it will not be necessary to cut a completely perfect circle shape.

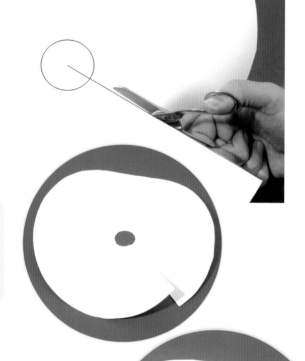

Cut along the straight line that you have traced between the two circumferences and the small circle in the centre.

13
Use the disc to form a cone that covers the wooden frame that you have built before.

14
Once you have completely molded the cone to the wooden structure, locate the spot where the straight line overlaps onto the thin cardboard. Looking at the picture will help you. Make a mark with a pencil on the exact spot where the straight line stops on the thin cardboard.

15
Along the mark that you have just made on the thin cardboard disc, draw a straight line that connects the outer part of the circle with the inner part.

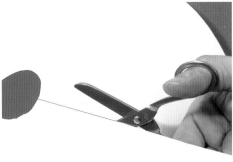

17

On a piece of cardboard
that is not very thick, trace
the fan shape of the disc.

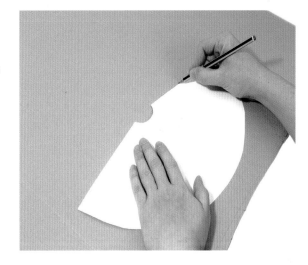

16

Using scissors, cut the disc along the line
that you have just drawn. Do it the same
way that you did with the first straight line
at the beginning of the project.

18

Using a cutter, cut out the fan shape
that you have just drawn on the
cardboard. To make this cut, you must
ask an adult to help you. Mark the
centre of the fan with the ruler and a
pencil.

19

Now, with the help of a ruler,
fold the cardboard fan along the
straight line that divides it down
the middle, as shown
in the picture.

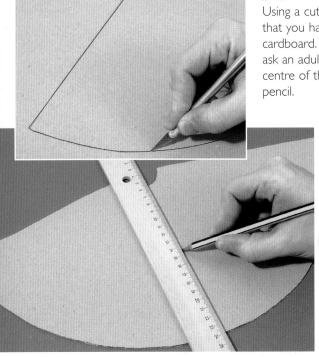

Indian Teepee

On the cardboard, trace a straight line along the stick, as shown in the picture, and do the same with the stick that is on the other side of the folding line in the middle of the cardboard.

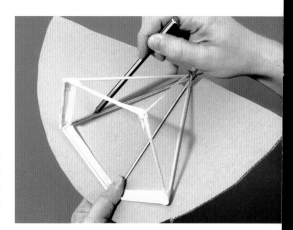

20

Place the frame inside the cardboard fan that you have just made. Do this by matching up one of the vertical sticks with the straight line along which you have folded the cardboard. Without moving the frame, mark the position of the stick that is next to the stick that lies on the folding line.

To make a nice fold, you must make sure that the ruler lies on the straight line and then press the ruler down forcefully while you fold the cardboard towards yourself.

24

Cover the wooden frame with the cardboard again, and mark the places for the wooden sticks that you have not yet marked.

22

Remove the cardboard from the frame and use a ruler and a pencil to draw a straight line over the places that you have just marked.

23

Using the ruler, and following the same process as before, fold the fan-shaped cardboard along the lines that you have just drawn.

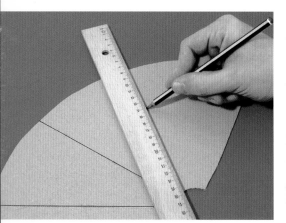

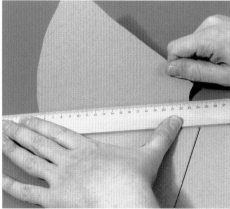

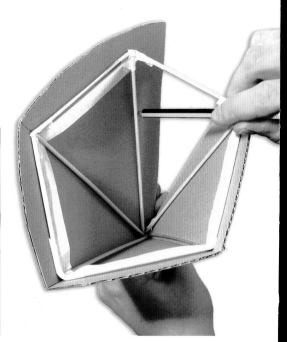

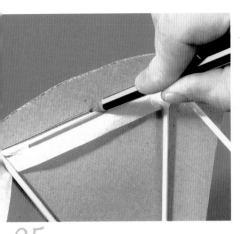

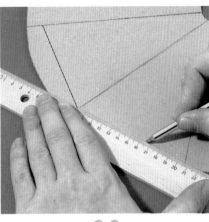

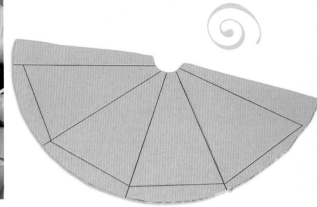

25

When you have marked all of the straight lines for the wooden frame, also mark the straight lines for the bottom of the teepee.

26

Using a ruler and a pencil, go over the marks which you have just made to make them totally straight.

Look at the shape that you have drawn on the cardboard fan. It is a uniform shape that we will use to imitate the triangular sides of an Indian teepee.

27

Using scissors, cut off the leftover cardboard around the fan. First cut the part that is leftover on the sides that you have drawn. Then cut off the leftover part underneath the marks that you have made along the sticks at the teepee base.

Once you have traced the marks, it is advisable that you go over the marks again with a ruler and pencil, so that the folding lines and cuts are correct.

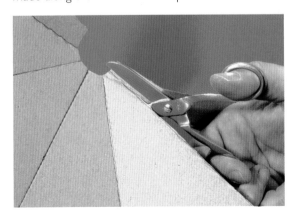

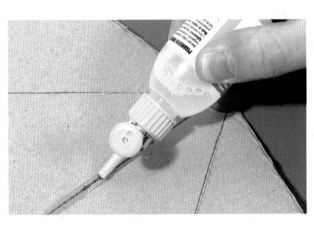

28

Now paste a little glue on the middle folding line where you are going to stick the wooden teepee frame.

61

Indian Teepee

29

After you have stuck the cardboard on the wooden frame, secure the wooden stick to the cardboard with a piece of adhesive tape that completely covers the stick.

Indians used geometric motifs to decorate their tents, and you can do the same thing.

Once you have stuck on all the sides of the teepee, secure the bottom of the teepee with a little more adhesive tape. Now your Indian teepee is ready to be painted!

30

With a soft-bristled paintbrush start painting each one of the triangle sides of the tent. Apply brushstrokes from top to bottom, so that the direction of the brushstrokes is in line with the vertical form of the teepee. When you have painted the outside, let the paint dry for a couple of hours.

With a little brown and white paint you will obtain a colour resembling buffalo hide. These Indian teepees were usually covered with buffalo hides, but we will have to make do with imitating this colour with paint.

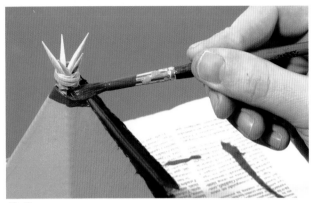

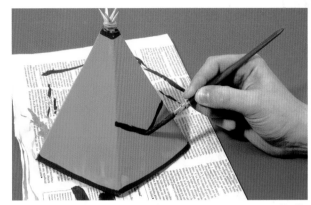

31

Once the paint is dry, start painting the side frame of the door with brown paint. Paint the sticks that make up the base of the tent, especially in the entrance. Also paint the top of the cardboard a little, as if you were outlining the edges of the hides on the tent.

32

Using the same brown paint, paint some lines about halfway up the tent. Paint a slanted line starting from one of the sides and ending at the centre of the triangle, as you can see in the picture. Repeat this process on all angles of the teepee.

33

With a decorated rubber stamp you can stamp figures on the sides of the tent. To do this, use bold and bright colours.

34

Decorate your teepee with a lot of colours. The more you use, the more fun and more original it will be!

35

Now you just need to find a place for your teepee at home, so that the Last Mohican or the Great Chief Sitting Bull can move into your teepee!